Chihuahuas

Everything You Need to Know about Pet
Chihuahuas

Chihuahua Characteristics, Health, Buying, Diet,
Breeding, Types, Showing, Care and a whole lot more!

By Lolly Brown

Foreword

Chihuahuas are without a doubt a Hollywood favorite! From several TV cameos to big blockbuster movies starring none other but their breed certainly made these adorable little creatures a hit in pop culture. They earned a reputation as the dog companion of the "rich and famous."

Chihuahuas are classified as a toy breed, they are very active, fun to be with and also a caring canine. They are recognized in many dog clubs including the AKC and the Kennel Club UK. They are also one of the top 10 most recommended pets by many dog experts and enthusiasts.

The breed is healthy in general and has quite a long lifespan; they're also low maintenance, and have great personalities. Aside from being incredibly cute and loving, Chihuahuas are also very adaptive to its environment, they won't have a problem adjusting to a new home as long as you provide them with adequate living condition and of course, lots of love!

Embark on a wonderful journey of having Chihuahuas as your loyal and A - List pet just like many Hollywood celebrities that came before you!

Table of Contents

Introduction

Chihuahuas are one of the oldest breed of dogs in America. In fact, some historians even say that Mexican royalties from many centuries ago used Chihuahuas as an early hot water bottle source, sort of like a kind of rubber bag containing hot water that you put on your stomach whenever you have a tummy ache! How weird is that right? These dogs was once a "mini – heater." Most dogs function as farmers or guard dogs of castles during early times but Chihuahuas used to be a source of heat! Now that's something!

Fortunately, their breed now evolved as one of America's (and the world's) favorite house pet! They are cute as a button and they love being pampered by their owners. No wonder why people love them!

You may not know this but Chihuahuas are the smallest breed of dog in the world – which makes them the "ultimate" lap dogs! Those large dark eyes will practically beg you to pick them up. Chihuahuas are also among the top 10 watch dogs recommended by experts. These dogs love to be with people, are very protective of their owners and require only a minimum grooming maintenance and exercise. They are very energetic pets, but can also be quite temperamental at times, which is why training and socialization at an early age is needed. If you have small children, it is not advisable to get Chihuahuas as pets because they are very fragile.

According to most dog owners, Chihuahuas have such a huge personality; what they lack in size they certainly make up for in character. Chihuahuas are an intelligent and cheeky breed that you will surely encounter if you choose to make them your dog companion. Like most small breeds, these dogs tend to have quite a long life – expectancy; they usually live for about 12 – 18 years! They might suffer from a small dog syndrome which is very common among miniature size breeds but generally these dogs are healthy.

Chihuahuas are also one, if not, the most popular dog breeds in media, fashion and entertainment! You'll see them being carried around by celebs and fashion icons. Sometimes they are also "hanging out" with VIPs and even walking on the red carpet at big time events. They have been featured in several TV shows and movies such as Legally Blonde and Beverly Hills Chihuahua. They are truly the definition of the rich and famous in Hollywood!

Before getting a pet, you must get to know the type of dog you will be getting. This book will help you in to getting to know a Chihuahua better. It will give you useful and helpful tips in taking care, training, feeding, socializing and dealing with them. Hopefully this book will make you the best Chihuahua owner you can be.

This book also includes information about showing your Chihuahuas as well as some health problems that an owner will commonly encounter. I am sure you are excited to get to know more about the Chihuahua breed, read on!

Glossary of Dog Terms

AKC – American Kennel Club, the largest purebred dog registry in the United States

Almond Eye – Referring to an elongated eye shape rather than a rounded shape

Apple Head – A round-shaped skull

Balance – A show term referring to all of the parts of the dog, both moving and standing, which produce a harmonious image

Beard – Long, thick hair on the dog's underjaw

Best in Show – An award given to the only undefeated dog left standing at the end of judging

Bitch – A female dog

Bite – The position of the upper and lower teeth when the dog's jaws are closed; positions include level, undershot, scissors, or overshot

Blaze – A white stripe running down the center of the face between the eyes

Board – To house, feed, and care for a dog for a fee

Breed – A domestic race of dogs having a common gene pool and characterized appearance/function

Breed Standard – A published document describing the look, movement, and behavior of the perfect specimen of a particular breed

Buff – An off-white to gold coloring

Clip – A method of trimming the coat in some breeds

Coat – The hair covering of a dog; some breeds have two coats, and outer coat and undercoat; also known as a double coat. Examples of breeds with double coats include German Shepherd, Siberian Husky, Akita, etc.

Condition – The health of the dog as shown by its skin, coat, behavior, and general appearance

Crate – A container used to house and transport dogs; also called a cage or kennel

Crossbreed (Hybrid) – A dog having a sire and dam of two different breeds; cannot be registered with the AKC

Dam (bitch) – The female parent of a dog;

Dock – To shorten the tail of a dog by surgically removing the end part of the tail.

Double Coat – Having an outer weather-resistant coat and a soft, waterproof coat for warmth; see above.

Drop Ear – An ear in which the tip of the ear folds over and hangs down; not prick or erect

Entropion – A genetic disorder resulting in the upper or lower eyelid turning in

Fancier – A person who is especially interested in a particular breed or dog sport

Fawn – A red-yellow hue of brown

Feathering – A long fringe of hair on the ears, tail, legs, or body of a dog

Groom – To brush, trim, comb or otherwise make a dog's coat neat in appearance

Heel – To command a dog to stay close by its owner's side

Hip Dysplasia – A condition characterized by the abnormal formation of the hip joint

Inbreeding – The breeding of two closely related dogs of one breed

Kennel – A building or enclosure where dogs are kept

Litter – A group of puppies born at one time

Markings – A contrasting color or pattern on a dog's coat

Mask – Dark shading on the dog's foreface

Mate – To breed a dog and a bitch

Neuter – To castrate a male dog or spay a female dog

Pads – The tough, shock-absorbent skin on the bottom of a dog's foot

Parti-Color – A coloration of a dog's coat consisting of two or more definite, well-broken colors; one of the colors must be white

Pedigree – The written record of a dog's genealogy going back three generations or more

Pied – A coloration on a dog consisting of patches of white and another color

Prick Ear – Ear that is carried erect, usually pointed at the tip of the ear

Puppy – A dog under 12 months of age

Purebred – A dog whose sire and dam belong to the same breed and who are of unmixed descent

Saddle – Colored markings in the shape of a saddle over the back; colors may vary

Shedding – The natural process whereby old hair falls off the dog's body as it is replaced by new hair growth.

Sire – The male parent of a dog

Smooth Coat – Short hair that is close-lying

Spay – The surgery to remove a female dog's ovaries, rendering her incapable of breeding

Trim – To groom a dog's coat by plucking or clipping

Undercoat – The soft, short coat typically concealed by a longer outer coat

Wean – The process through which puppies transition from subsisting on their mother's milk to eating solid food

Whelping – The act of birthing a litter of puppies

Chapter One: Chihuahuas in Focus

The Chihuahua breed is recognized by American Kennel Club (AKC) and the Kennel Club UK. Since it is a recognized breed, it has certain physical characteristics that must pass the given standard. Chihuahua's are expected to have a height proportioned to its body length and its head. This breed is also very competitive when it comes to dog shows! Chihuahuas are known as active and athletic pets, but of course that is not the only thing that describes it. They are very loyal, cheerful and also witty. They are among the most intelligent breeds of dogs in the world and despite their size they have a huge personality that can certainly fill up a room!

Before you decide whether or not it might be the right pet for you and your family, you need to learn and invest a significant amount of time in getting to know the "basic stuff" about your chosen breed. In this chapter, you will learn about basic Chihuahua facts and information, as well as the history of how it came about. This information, in combination with the succeeding information in the next chapters will help you decide if Chihuahua's are the perfect dog companion for you.

Facts about Chihuahua

No one exactly knows where Chihuahuas came from; some say that it was a descendant of a companion dog called Techichi that originally came from Mexico during the Toltec Civilization. There are a lot of myths and folklores surrounding the origins of Chihuahuas but there's still no evidence supporting various claims.

The Chihuahua is a graceful, alert and cute dog with a 'saucy' expression. These dogs weigh about 3 – 6 pounds and has a height of 15 – 23 cm on average (but sometimes vary depending on the type of breed – more on this later) that's why their size makes them awesome dogs especially for people living in small – city apartments or even in studio – type dormitories; they can basically live in your own bedroom and be more than contented with it (as long as it is adequate).

Chihuahuas come in two types of coat; they could be short – coated or long – coated. Both coat types can be any solid color or it could also have a variety of markings and patches of other colors in some parts of their body. They come in Tan, Red, Black, White or Splashed coats.

Their heads can either be an Apple or deer shaped. They also have the largest brain among dog breeds in the entire planet! They are small but certainly incredible.

These dogs are very adaptable to any kind of environment but they should strictly live inside a home or an apartment because they're in – house kind of dogs. Chihuahuas are also good travellers and can easily go anywhere with their owners; since they are classified as a toy breed, they can be easily carried. They are very light and perhaps a really handy and "portable" kind of pet.

Even if this canine is miniature, never underestimate them because they still have that terrier - like attitude. It's very common among mini breeds like Chihuahuas to have quite a tenacious personality. They are indeed sweet, loyal and protective but they can also be witty, and will not let anything stop them. If you do not train them well and socialize them with other house pets, you might end up raising a little tyrant!

If you don't want a noisy or crazy dog, then a Chihuahua may not be the pet for you. They tend to bark a lot, and they are also very prone to nipping and biting someone if you do not train them properly.

When it comes to shedding, they do not shed a lot compare to other toy breed dogs. They are quite easy to groom and only needs 30 minutes to 1 hour exercise every day. They are also not picky eaters, they'll pretty much eat whatever food you put in front of them, just make sure that you don't overfeed them because it can cause obesity. Proper nutrition is needed, which will also be tackled later on in this book.

Like any other dogs, they are also pre - disposed to certain illnesses such as small dog syndrome, hypoglycemia, obesity and other diseases and conditions common among miniature breeds. Nevertheless, they are pretty much long – term pets that could last for about 12 – 18 years, sometimes even more provided that you give them proper nutrition and adequate living environment – not to mention lots of attention!

On the next sections, you will be provided with summary of facts and also a bit of history on how these adorable pets came about.

Summary of Chihuahua Facts

Pedigree: Toy Breed

Breed Size: Small

Height: 15 – 23 cm (5 – 9 inches) tall

Weight: weighs 1.5 – 3 kg (3 – 6 pounds)

Types: Smooth-Coat Chihuahua; Long-Coat Chihuahua; Apple Head Chihuahua; Deer Head Chihuahua; Teacup Chihuahua; Fawn Chihuahua

Coat Texture: may be smooth and silky

Color: Tan, Red, Black, White or Splashed

Eyes: bulging eyes that is dark and expressive

Ears: erect ears when matured or full grown; drop ears when younger

Tail: erect and curled up; about 3 - 5 inches in length

Temperament: can be easily trained, intelligent, tenacious, active, loyal, sweet

Strangers: sociable when trained well, but are not that welcoming.

Other Dogs: proper socialization is needed. They could have barking tendencies and also tend to always throw themselves at larger dogs

Other Pets: generally not good with other pets

Training: Highly trainable

Exercise Needs: requires minimum exercise and play time with the use of lively activities; about 30 minutes to about an hour a day

Health Conditions: generally healthy but may be prone to certain health conditions such as Hydrocephalus, Hypoglycemia, Patellar Luxation, Tracheal Collapse, Obesity, Hip Dysplasia and Cataracts.

Lifespan: average 12 - 18 years or more

Chihuahua Breed History

Chihuahuas are believed to have originated from Mexico. I say, "believe" because historians cannot pinpoint on where exactly they came from or who their ancestors are, unlike other dog breeds. However, based from several myths, folklore stories and archaeological findings, there is one common place where these adorable creatures may have originated – Mexico. The most common theory is that Chihuahuas are descendants of a companion dog in Mexico called Techichi during the Toltec Civilization. Though there were no historical evidences to prove it, archaeologists dug some materials inside the Great Pyramid of Cholula that may have come from a Chihuahua breed around 1530. As a matter of fact, dog toys representing both deer head and apple head (two head varieties of Chihuahuas) were found from Mexico to El Salvador that dates back to about 100 A.D.

In 1850, a deer – head shaped Chihuahua ruin was found in Casas Grandes at the Mexican state of Chihuahua. The ruins date back to 1100 – 1300 A.D. which only shows the possible long history of the breed in Mexico.

Chihuahuas were believed to be "spirit guides," and were used during rituals by native Aztecs in Mexico before the Spaniards arrive. Some people also believe that Chihuahuas could be one of the first native dogs in the Americas while others think that they may have descended from Pariah dogs. Nevertheless, the breed's name is taken from the state of Mexico.

Today, the Chihuahua we know were developed by North American breeders. In 1904, the first Chihuahua called Midget was officially registered in the AKC. In 1923, the Chihuahua Club of America was established. According to the AKC, the Chihuahuas ranks 13th among the most popular breeds in the world.

Chapter Two: Chihuahuas' Requirements

Getting a dog is not just getting a breed that you've heard about, or what is popular, or what your neighbor has. There is such a thing as compatibility of a pet to its dog owner. Not every dog is the right dog for you. You have to make sure that it fits you, your family and the environment that you have.

This chapter contains information about the pros and cons of having a Chihuahua breed as a pet. You will also learn the average associated costs, and licensing which is required for you to become a legitimate Chihuahua owner if you decided to be one.

Do You Need a License?

There are certain regulations and restrictions that should be taken in to consideration when purchasing a dog, or in this case Chihuahua. Acquiring a license for your pets can be different depending on the country, state and region that you are in.

In the United States, there is no federal requirement for getting a license for your pets, but it is the State that regulars these kinds of rules. Though it is not required for you dogs to get a license, it is important that you do so. It will not just provide a protection for your pet, but also to you as a pet owner. An identification number is placed in your dog licensed which is directly linked to your contact details as the owner. This can be very helpful in case your pet gets lost.

It is important to take note that before you can get your dog a license, you must be vaccinated against rabies. This is the only requirement for you to acquire a license. Dog license are renewable every year which means that you have to get another rabies vaccination.

How Many Chihuahua's Should You Keep?

It is advisable to keep one Chihuahua per home. As mentioned in previews sections, Chihuahua requires a lot of time and attention when it comes to training and socialization. It will be hard for you to train a lot of Chihuahua especially if you are a first time dog owner. However, if you think you can handle their energy and loud personality, then of course, you are more than welcome to own as many Chihuahuas as you like, after all they are really adorable and they might appreciate a company of their own breed.

Owning more than one breed is still up to you as the pet owner since it will take a significant amount of effort in giving them all their needs. You have to consider their physical daily needs, as well as the time and affection that are vital for their growth and development. You must be willing to give your best effort in all the aspects of your life when you decide to get a dog.

Do Chihuahuas Get Along with Other Pets?

This breed may or may not get along with other pets because of many factors; sometimes if Chihuahuas are with larger dog breeds, they tend to throw themselves towards bigger dogs because they think they are invincible. Chihuahuas also tend to be tenacious and very active which could make other pets feel intimidated when they are around them, or it could also trigger other pets to quarrel with your Chihuahua. Fortunately, through proper training and socialization, your Chihuahuas might get along with your other household animals though supervision is highly recommended.

How Much Does it Cost to Keep a Chihuahuas?

Acquiring a dog is the easiest part but raising them is not! It entails a lot of responsibilities as a pet owner; owning a pet does not come cheap because you need to provide for their needs to make sure that they grow up healthy and reach their life expectancy. This section is an overview of the expenses of owning a Chihuahua. The expenses listed below include veterinary care, food and treats, toys, grooming and cleaning supplies. This can help you determine whether your pocket is ready for owning a pet.

Initial Costs

The average cost in purchasing a Chihuahua from a reputable breeder is about $850 – $1,550. It is important to buy from a reputable breeder because it will save you money and effort from getting a dog that has a lot of health issues. Other initial cost to factor in includes crate, leash and color, initial vaccination, licensing, spay/neuter and grooming supplies. Prices may vary on different locations, but below is an average of each of the initial purchase cost:

Initial Costs Overview

Initial Needs	Cost
Purchase Price	$850 – $1,550
Spaying or Neutering	$200
Medical Examination	$70 - $100
Crate	$50
Vaccination	$75
Leash and Collar	$30
Grooming Supplies	$35
Total	$1,310 – $2,040

*Cost may change depending on the brand, availability and location

*Cost also vary depending on the current exchange rate

Having a pet is very similar to raising a child. There is really a need for you to spend money to take good care of them and maintain your pet. These expenses will surely add up to your everyday expenditure, but it's part of being a responsible pet owner. Remember that providing your dog's needs is also a way of showing your love and affection for them.

Monthly Costs

The monthly costs associated with keeping a Chihuahua can also be quite expensive. Some of the things that need to be bought on a monthly basis are food and treats, annual license renewal, toy replacements, and veterinary exams. Provided in this section is an overview of each of these costs as well as an estimate for each cost.

Food and Treats: total of $50

Feeding your Chihuahua a healthy diet is very important for its health and wellness, especially for a very active and clever pet. A high-quality diet for dogs may not be cheap and it also highly depends on the brand. The right amount of nutrients should be provided to maintain its healthy and appealing physique. You should be prepared to spend around $40 for a high-quality dog food which will last you about a month. You should also include a monthly budget of at least $10 for treats, that way he/she can be rewarded every time he/she did a good job in training or behaving.

Grooming Costs: approximately $10.50

You should plan to have your Chihuahua professionally groomed about twice a year (depends on how much your dog sheds) in order to keep his skin and coat in good health. You should budget about $10.50 per month.

License Renewal: average of $2.00

The cost to license your Chihuahua is generally about $20 and you can renew the license for the same price each year, some states may cost more. License renewal cost divided over 12 months is about $2 per month.

Veterinary Exams: approximately $7.00

In order to keep your Chihuahua healthy you should take him to the veterinarian at least twice a year; keep in mind that you may need to take him more often while he is a puppy to give him the vaccines he needs. The average cost for a vet visit is about $40, if you have two visits per year, it averages to about $7 per month.

Additional Costs: $15

In addition to the cost for food, grooming, license renewal, and vet visits you will have to cover other costs on occasion. These costs may include replacements for toys, a larger collar as your puppy grows (some Chihuahua are over 6 pounds), cleaning products, and more. You won't have to cover these costs every month but you should include it in your budget to be safe.

An overview of these costs is provided for you in on the next section. Costs may vary depending on brand as well as location and the current exchange rate.

Monthly Expenses Overview

Needs	Monthly Costs
Food and Treats	$50
Grooming Costs	$10.50
License Renewal	$2
Veterinary Exams	$7
Other Costs	$15
Total	$84.50

Having a pet will greatly affect your spending that is why it is important to know if you are willing to adjust your budget. It is better to have an idea of what you should be expecting when it comes to owning a dog. Below is an average annual breakdown cost of owning one Chihuahua as can be seen in the table:

Needs	Annual Costs
Food expenses	Approximately $600
Veterinarian Exams/ Vaccinations	Approximately $984
Other costs (toys, treats and other accessories)	Approximately $1,140
Grooming	Approximately $126
Licensing	Approximately $20
Total	$2,870

What are the Pros and Cons of Chihuahua?

Before choosing a pet, it is important that you get to know them first. Every dog is different, every breed is unique. That is the reason why it is important to get to know them first by doing some research. This can help you decide whether a certain breed is suitable for you.

This section contains a list of pros and cons in having a Chihuahua as a pet. This can help you determine whether this breed fits you well.

Pros for Chihuahua

Get this type of breed…

- If you are not a first time dog owner and you have a lot of patience in training dogs
- If you can handle an energetic dog
- If you want an adorable and popular dog
- If you want a miniature - sized dog
- If you want a fun, loyal and loving dog
- If you are fond of petting a dog
- If you like a pet that is low maintenance
- If you like a pet that doesn't shed a lot
- If you like a healthy and long – term dog companion

Cons for Chihuahua

- They are challenging to train and socialize at first
- They have a very dynamic temperament which makes them hard to handle if not properly trained. T
- They can get vigilant and quite tenacious at times.

- They might tend to destroy things if they are not properly house trained.
- They can be aggressive towards other dogs and pets
- They bark excessively and are loud pets

Chapter Three: Purchasing a Chihuahua

After reading and learning about the basic facts of Chihuahuas, the next step is to know where and how to acquire this kind of breed. As a pet owner, you should be well - aware on where you will be getting your pet to ensure that the canine you will get is free from illnesses. This chapter will tackle tips on how to find a reputable breeder, where to get a healthy Chihuahua, and how to select healthy pups. You will also be provided with a list of Chihuahua breeders and websites as well as information regarding rescue adoption.

Finding a Reputable Chihuahua Breeder

Once you've decided that the Chihuahua is the right dog for you, your next step is to find one. Purchasing a Chihuahua might be as easy as stopping in to your local pet store since it is such a popular breed, but you should ask yourself whether this is really the best option. Many pet stores receive their puppies from puppy mills. Puppy mills are organizations that breed lots of dogs in the quickest time possible, keeping the dogs in squalid conditions. As a result of irresponsible breeding practices, the puppies are often malnourished or suffering from health problems. The best way to make sure you get a Chihuahua puppy in good health is to do your research and to purchase one from a reputable Chihuahua breeder.

Tips in Choosing a Reputable Breeder

The difference between a reputable breeder and a puppy producer is that the former spends large amounts of time and money on the best interest of the breed, while the latter is often motivated by profit. However, in order to find a good Chihuahua breeder, you may have to do some research first. Once you've compiled a list of several Chihuahua breeders you then need to go through them to choose the best option. You don't want to run the risk of purchasing a puppy from a hobby breeder or from someone who doesn't follow responsible breeding practices. Keep in mind that when you purchase a Chihuahua puppy you are making an 18 year commitment!

Here are the following things you need to do to help you find a reputable Chihuahua breeder:

- Ask around at veterinary offices, groomers, and pet stores for referrals to Chihuahua breeders and assemble as much information as you can about each one.

- Visit the website for each breeder (if they have one) and check to see if the breeder is registered with a national or local breed club

- Contact each breeder individually and ask them questions about their knowledge of the Chihuahua breed as well as their breeding experience.

- Ask specific questions about the breeder's program and the dogs used to produce the puppies. Ask what the breeder does to prevent the passing of congenital conditions to the puppies.

- Remove the breeders from your list who do not seem to be knowledgeable about the breed or if they seem to be just hobby breeders looking to make a buck.

- Eliminate breeders from your list who refuse to answer your questions or who do not seem genuinely concerned for the wellbeing of their puppies.

- Schedule a visit with several breeders and ask for a tour of the facilities – check to make sure they are clean and that the dogs look healthy.

- Narrow down your list of breeders and make your selection – you should also ask about the breeder's preferences for putting down a deposit on a puppy.

- Place your deposit to reserve a puppy – in the next section you will receive tips for choosing a puppy from a litter.

Rescue Dogs Adoption

As an alternative to purchasing a Chihuahua puppy from a legitimate breeder, you should also consider adopting a rescue dog. Not only will you be doing your part in the war against puppy mills, but you will be providing a homeless dog with a loving home and new lease on life. There are many benefits associated with adopting a rescue dog and you might even be able to find a purebred Chihuahua puppy.

Adoption is much more affordable than purchasing a purebred puppy from a breeder and the dog is likely to have already been housebroken and may also have some amount of obedience training as well.

List of Breeders and Rescue Websites

In this section, you'll be given recommended websites on reputable breeders as well as rescue dogs associations in United States and United Kingdom, once you have narrow down your list of breeders, you can go and check to see the best option for you.

Chihuahua Breeders

AKC Marketplace

<http://marketplace.akc.org/puppies/chihuahua>

Puppy Spot

<https://www.puppyspot.com/breed/chihuahua/?breed_id=2 19>

Kennel Club Assured Breeders

<https://www.thekennelclub.org.uk/services/public/acbr/Default.aspx?breed=Chihuahua+(Smooth+Coat)>

Chielle Chihuahuas

<http://chielleshowchis.webs.com/>

Tiny Haven Chihuahuas

<http://tinyhavenchis.weebly.com/ >

Las Vegas Chihuahuas

<http://lasvegastinychihuahua.webs.com/>

TK Ranch Chihuahua

<http://www.tkranchchihuahua.com/>

House of Chi's

<http://www.houseofchis.com/>

PetchiDog

<http://www.petchidog.com/chihuahua-breeders>

Bonbon Chihuahuas
<http://www.chihuahuapuppiesakc.com/chihuahua_puppies_for_sale/>

Dogzonline (Australia)

<https://www.dogzonline.com.au/breeds/breeders/chihuahua-smooth-coat.asp>

SunGold Chihuahuas

<http://www.indianachihuahuas.com/>

Cartens Chihuahuas

<http://www.carstenschihuahuas.com/>

Misti's Chihuahuas

<http://mistischihuahuas.homestead.com/>

Badgercrest

<https://www.badgercrest.com/>

Rescue Adoption

Texas Chihuahua Rescue

<http://texaschihuahuarescue.com/>

Chihuahua - Rescue

<http://www.chihuahua-rescue.com/http://www.chihuahua-rescue.com/>

Chihuahua Rescue Australia

<http://chihuahuarescueaustralia.com/>

Adopt – a – Pet

<http://www.adoptapet.com/s/adopt-a-chihuahua>

Chihuahua & Small Dog Rescue

<http://www.chihuahua-smalldogrescue.org/>

Chihuahua Rescue Victoria (Australia)

<http://www.chihuahuarescuevictoria.org/>

Chihuahua Rescue Indiana

<http://chihuahuarescuein.org/>

Chihuahua Rescue of San Diego

<http://chihuahuarescueofsandiego.com/>

BC Chihuahua Rescue

<http://chirescue.org/>

Tips on Purchasing a Chihuahua

Your chosen Chihuahua will be part of your family for an extended period so make sure to select the right dog for your family. Remember to not impulsively purchase that cute puppy in the window of your local pet shop to avoid many of the problems experienced by new puppy owners and save yourself a lot of heartaches. If you want to own a pet, escape from impulse buying.

It is recommended to purchase your Chihuahua puppy from a trusted and reputable breeder or preferably a registered show breeder. It is very simple to select a dedicated breeder; just ask if either the parent of the Chihuahua is a champion and how many wins the breeder has bred. Also, ask the number of years the breeder has been showing their Chihuahua. This will give you the best opportunity of obtaining a companion who is a true representative of its breed. Never be fooled into purchasing a Chihuahua from a registered backyard breeder. It is recommended that you must research the Chihuahua breed thoroughly before buying.

The following are the questions you should ask the breeder before buying a Chihuahua from a breeder:

- Ask to see and visit the puppy and the parents in the breeder's home.

- Ask to see both the parents because this will give you an idea of how the puppy will be as an adult. Do not buy a Chihuahua from a breeder that refuses to allow you to come to their place and see the parents of the Chihuahua.

- If you are buying online, ask for more photos of the puppy at different angles to make sure it is not a scam. Also, ask to forward the photos of the parents to you.

- Ask questions about the size of the Chihuahua. A good breeder can tell you the puppies' current weight.

- Ask about any health problems. Has the Chihuahua been vet checked? Are they wormed on regular basis? Has the Chihuahua been micro chipped?

- Ask if the parents of the puppy are DNA profiled.

- Ask if the breeder has been involved in Chihuahua rescue. Only purchase a puppy from a breeder who is dedicated to the breed.

- Ask if the breeder belongs to a Breed Club or Association. In the United States, puppies should be registered with the AKC (American Kennel Club), while in the UK it's called the Kennel Club.

- Take note, it's highly recommended that you purchase AKC/Kennel Club registry puppies. This is because these organizations have strict rules of requirements and membership from the breeders. This rule is a good safeguard for dog buyers.

- Ask if the breeder has a contract. A reputable breeder will have a contract that must detail out all conditions of sale.

- Ask if the breeder has a website. Most good breeders have a website. Also, be sure to avoid breeders who offer credit card or other easy payment methods online, including PayPal. Beware of the breeders who are in a hurry to sell their pet and close the deal.

If you are really interested in purchasing a Chihuahua dog, whether it is an adult or a puppy, do not hesitate to visit the Chihuahua directory provided on the AKC and the Kennel Club UK websites. It lists the very best Chihuahua breeders, AKC Registered Chihuahua Breeders and Reputable Kennel Clubs.

Selecting a Healthy Chihuahua

Chihuahuas are generally a healthy dog breed, however, like any other canine, they are predisposed to illnesses which is why you must be aware that your dog is healthy so that it won't be difficult to take care of them.

Keeping an eye for early signs of medical problems of your dog is of utmost importance; it could save you a lot of stress, time and money in the long run – not to mention your dog's health. This section will give you information if your Chihuahua dog is healthy to keep.

- **Check its Body and Overall Appearance**

You should be doing a full body check on your potential dog. You can gently run your hand over all the parts of the dog's body and check for cuts, lumps, inflammation and any signs of discomfort.

- **Observe on their walking/activities**

Watch the way the dogs move and how it interacts with other puppies. Observe how he walks and runs. Does he ever seem stiff? Get easily tired? Or have a limp? Excessive panting and coughing may also indicate problems

- **Check their weight**

  The Chihuahua should not be obese or underweight for its size. If you think the pups are too fat or too thin then that means the breeders are not properly feeding them.

- **Check their mouth**

  Check your potential dog's mouth for anything out of the ordinary. Gums must be pink. If you see darker/redder patches, it may indicate a problem. You must also check for growths and lumps, and make sure that the teeth are clear. Observe also their breath as unusually bad breath could be an indication of digestive problems.

- **Check their eyes**

  Eyes of dogs should be clear and the pupils should be of the same size. Check for ingrowing hair or eye lashes that look like it's causing a problem. Make sure also that there is no excessive discharge or signs of irritation.

- **Check their nose and ears**

  The nose of dogs should be cool and moist. Keep an eye out for excessive sneezing, discharge and make sure that breathing is unobstructed and easy. You should also check the ears of the dog for wax build-up, bad odor, and swelling.

- **Check their private area**

Lastly, check if their private parts don't have any signs of swelling or redness to ensure that they don't have any reproductive problems or internal problems.

Chapter Four: Caring Guidelines for Chihuahua

It is important that when you get a pet, you must have the willingness to care of it at all cost. The Chihuahua breed could be quite challenging because you need a lot of patience to tame and train them, fortunately, they are smart and active dog breed that's why it will also be fun and education for you as the trainer. Properly caring for your pet can be both a beneficial and rewarding experience. It will surely bring out the best in you and your pet. This chapter will teach you on how to properly socialize and train your Chihuahuas. Housebreaking tips are also provided as well as other caring guidelines for your adorable dog.

Socializing Your Dog

The best time to socialize your Chihuahua is when they are, in fact, a pup. Dogs are at their most receptive and sensitive between three and twelve weeks of age. The earlier you can get your dog socialized, the better. After those span of twelve weeks, it can be very difficult to get a puppy to accept anything unfamiliar.

- **Walk your dog daily**

  Dog walks have a great advantage in meeting new dogs and people. It's also a great practice for them to show them proper behavior when they are out, because you're just bound to run into more social situations when your dog is out for a walk than when staying at home. Chihuahuas loves to run around!

- **Use a muzzle when other dogs come over**

  If you already know that your Chihuahua barks or growls at other dogs, it can help if you let them use a muzzle. This prevents the danger of attacking or biting and it can also make the dogs calmer so they'll be more sensitive to meeting other dogs and have a more positive experience.

- **Expose your dogs to different social activities**

If you can introduce your dog to a new activity once a week, it will go a long way in helping them socialize, be calm and more behaved.

Training Your Chihuahuas

The good thing about Chihuahua is that they are very good with training; whether it is for heeling, housebreaking or performing tricks. They are one of the most intelligent dog breeds in the world, so training will be a piece of cake for them!

Training is a combined effort between the owner and the dog. You as the owner will take the important role of a teacher, and of course, your Chihuahua hopefully will be a great student. Chihuahuas are pretty fast learners but it may take longer based on some other factors like inconsistency or not having enough time during training.

Two of the most important things to be considered are first, how strictly you will to stick with the training or training schedule. The second is your strategy on how you can get your pet to behave during training, and make it enjoyable for them at the same time.

A lot of these things depend on you, which is why it's essential to understand and follow housebreaking guidelines. On the next section, you will learn several training tips and behavior guidelines to ensure that your Chihuahua is well – behaved.

Potty training

A lot of owners believe that toy breed dogs can easily be trained to use a litter box or pee pads. This is not as easy as it sounds, but it is still possible. Chihuahua's may have a hard time using pee pads because they have a natural instinct to want to choose on the right spot to pee or poop.

However, indoor training can be easily done if you are persistent and if you have a cooperative Chihuahua. There should be a chosen spot as the 'designated bathroom area' inside the house. Make sure to always make them pee and poo in the same spot so that they can easily remember it and also get used to it. You'll be surprise at how fast they can learn simple things like this.

Preparing to Housebreak Your Chihuahua

- **Choose a containment method**

A Chihuahua that is not fully housebroken should never be free in either a room or the house especially if he is not well - supervised because they can trash your apartment real quick even if they are small in size.

- **Choose your reward treats**

A Chihuahua is going to be more motivated to focus in behaving properly, learn more during training, understand that he did something right, and look forward to the next training lesson if he is properly rewarded with treats.

- **Be ready for a speedy exit**

To have your Chihuahua wearing his collar and to keep the leash right by the door is the final step in preparing to facilitate a fast exit to the designated area. It is highly recommended to have a harness. If you are not used to having one, you may at first think that they are difficult to take on and off, as you go along of course, it will become easier.

You are already ready to housebreak your Chihuahua successfully once you...

- Have chosen the best location for your dog's designated bathroom area that will be relatively easy to reach.
- Have set up a playpen or some other containment method for your dog to be at any time you can't keep an eye on him
- Have special training treats right by the exit door and have your dog's harness on him and his leash that is ready to spring into action

Housebreaking Tips

- Keep your Chihuahua with you, as often as possible. If he will pee or poo, clap your hand loudly or call out his name to cause him to pause.
- Your prep should allow you to exit with your dog quickly, but carry him if needed.
- As your Chihuahua is doing the deed, repeat a chosen word or phrase so that he can associate it with his actions. Some owners use 'bathroom' or 'piddy potty'.
- Bring your Chihuahua outside with a specific schedule. If you are heading to the yard to get some exercise, bring him to his bathroom area first.

- Allow your Chihuahua at least 15 minutes to find the perfect spot within the area, and for his bladder and bowel muscles to relax.
- If your Chihuahua is done peeing in the right spot, offer the reward treat right away. Always give praise to them at the same time.
- If your Chihuahua misses the 'bathroom area,' don't punish him or her right away. They'll eventually learn in their own time. Make sure to clean the area with an enzyme cleanser.

Behavioral Problems

Active, intelligent, and a relatively healthy breed, Chihuahuas make a great companion and also do well in competitions, including obedience and agility trials. Some Chihuahuas may be prone to specific behavioral problems, so potential owners should consider the temperament of these dogs before adopting one.

Aggression and Fear

Chihuahuas tend to be suspicious around strangers and they become intimidated to large people and animals because of their small size. Fear can turn to aggression and you should not consider your dog's fear as an endearing behavior.

Possessiveness and Territoriality

Chihuahuas are also likely to be possessive of toys and food because they have 'tyrannistic' tendencies. You should train them by putting your hand in their bowl and playing toy exchange games when she is a puppy. This will decrease the likelihood of territorial behavior in adulthood

Excessive barking

Chihuahuas are notoriously yappy dogs, especially when they are not socialized to strangers and loud noises. You can put your dog in a crate when they bark excessively loud and reward them for being calm and quiet when there are visitors.

Grooming Chihuahua Dogs

Chihuahuas are low maintenance when it comes to grooming. Of course, if grooming is not performed properly or on a regular basis, things can go out of control. The coat can become matted. Fur may become brittle. The skin may dry out. Tear stains might become excessive. Paws and nose might peel. In short, it can become a disaster. Chihuahuas don't shed too much compare to other dogs but you still need to check their grooming status every once in a while.

Regular Chihuahua Grooming Tips

- **Toenails**

  Make sure to clip your Chihuahua's toenails with dog toenail clippers once every six or eight weeks. It will keep your dog's paws clean and healthy and will prevent him from scratching upon jumping up. Be sure not to cut their nails too close as this may hurt them.

- **Teeth**

  You have to thoroughly brush your Chihuahua's teeth on a regular basis so that they won't get dental cavities. You have to use special toothpaste that contains enzymes to inhibit bacterial growth in the mouth.

- **Eyes**

  Chihuahua's bulging round eyes can potentially have an eye discharge that may cause an infection due to bacteria. Hence, it is important to clean the eye area of your Chihuahua.

- **Trimming**

Your Chihuahua does not need to be shaved down during hot weather. There is no reason to shave your Chihuahua's beautiful coat just because the weather is hot. Little touch-ups to keep things clean and neat can be done every 2 to 3 months or as needed.

Show Dog Chihuahua Training

You can go far beyond basic commands in training a Chihuahua if you are committed; these dogs are very well known for their exceptional learning skills. This makes them an ideal breed for the show ring.

The following information will give you an idea on how to use the right Chihuahua training to prepare your pet in becoming a show dog.

- You need to understand that training for a show requires a lot of hard work because the lessons are much complicated than basic housebreaking training.

- You should learn how to properly groom your Chihuahua for a show. You can get it from a professional book, from a video or from a groomer itself. You should make grooming an enjoyable experience just like dog training. It will surely help get your Chihuahua used to grooming because this will help him become more accustomed to being handled.

- Practice posing or stacking your dog as soon as he is comfortable with the grooming table. First, have him stay in his position for a few seconds. And then increase the time you make him stay on the table. Be sure to give him a lot of rewards for standing poised for a long period of time.

Once your dog knows how to stay poised, you can move to the next step of his training which is the inspecting your Chihuahua as a judge will.
You have to check his legs, teeth, feet etc.

- You can enroll your Chihuahua in handling classes
- Your dog will need leash training. This form of training is about putting him on a leash and then eventually allowing him to go wherever he wants.

Once your Chihuahua is already familiar with changing directions, the next thing is to teach him on a loose head. Your dog will be taught to stand beside you when you stop, and then your dog will walk beside you, right or left side.

- You can also attend conformation training classes. These are to mirror show conditions, which make them an ideal place for show training. These classes will surely help you learn and fine tune all the skills that are required in a show ring.

Finally, before deciding to enter your Chihuahua in a dog show, you should first attend a few shows so you can have an idea. The more you and your dog are prepared for a show, the more your training will pay off.

Chapter Five: Nutritional Needs of Chihuahua Dogs

Providing proper nutrition for your Chihuahua is very essential in his overall health. Chihuahua puppies need the right amount of nutrition to grow, adults need the best diet to maintain health and seniors need the right food to meet the needs of an aging body. Just like humans, dogs need to be taken care of especially on the food they eat because it is a huge contributing factor in their life expectancy. As an owner, it's your duty to keep them fed up!

This section will elaborate all the tips on how to feed your Chihuahua and the basic nutritional needs that they require in order to have a healthy immune system

Tips for Feeding Your Chihuahua

Different foods have different amounts of calories so the recommended serving size will also vary. The right amount of food that a Chihuahua requires will vary on his age, activity level, and individual metabolism.

The recommended servings for puppies are 55 calories per pound while for adult Chihuahuas are 45 calories per pound. When your Chihuahua is in labor, her appetite may increase and if she appears to want more after finishing his meal, do not hesitate to offer a second serving. However, make sure that it's not too much, offer it in moderation.

Protein

Chihuahuas obviously have a tiny stomach which means that they cannot properly digest foods with a lot of filler especially that most dog food companies use grain and plant matter as filler in their foods. Chihuahuas that do not get enough proteins may become malnourished and underweight. If you choose to buy commercial canned food, it should contain little to no filler. You can let your dog eat small amounts of boiled chicken or liver but be sure that it is cooked, as puppies' stomachs are not developed enough to digest raw food.

Dry Food

Tooth loss is very common for miniature toy breeds like Chihuahuas so in order to prevent it, you need to provide dry dog food which will keep your dog's teeth and gums healthy. Dry dog food to be chosen should be in small pieces so that it will be easy for tiny mouths to chew.

Treats

You cannot easily give your Chihuahua too many treats as a tiny dog has a tiny stomach. Always remember that dogs in general should not eat foods or treats that people eat such as chocolates, gums etc. You can give your Chihuahua commercial treats for as long as there is no filler. This can serve as occasional treats or for positive reinforcement in training.

Types of Commercial Dog Foods

In this section, we will discuss the three main types of commercial dog foods. They can either be wet food, soft/moist, and dry foods. They are different in many aspects including moisture content, palatability, cost, and nutritional benefit.

- **Soft or Moist Food**

This is usually sold in boxes and contains single-serving pouches. It contains approximately 15 - 25% protein, 5 - 10% fat, 25 - 35% carbohydrates, and approximately 30% water. This type of food is highly palatable and very convenient to serve and store.

- **Wet food**

Wet foods are usually sold in cans and contain 75 to 80 % water, 8 - 15% protein and 2 - 15% fat. Dogs eat more of this type of food without gaining weight because of the high moisture content. Canned foods, if compared to dry and soft/moist products offer the highest palatability, but wet food also has the highest cost per serving,

- **Dry Food**

Dry foods are packed in bags and contain 18 - 40% protein, 7 - 22% fat, 12 - 50% carbohydrates and about 10% moisture. It comes in different sizes, shapes, and colors because dog discerns the density, texture, shape and size of the food, and the way food may feel in the mouth contributes to palatability.

How Often to Feed Chihuahuas

The number of meals that you give to a Chihuahua depends on his age. Feeding your dog the right amount of food can also be tricky. Below, you will know how much to feed your pet depending on his age.

- **Brand new puppies**

It is recommended to free-feed during the first month of your Chihuahua, meaning, fresh food is left out at all times. This is because blood sugar can drop quickly for young puppies, and one cause of this is not eating enough amount of food.

- **Puppies 3 months to 12 months**

  In this age range, you must feed your puppy three times a day. You may consider buying a treat dispensing toy so that if you will be gone during the day for the mid-meal, your Chihuahua will not miss his food.

- **Adult and Senior Dogs**

  Some adult Chihuahuas are good with eating three times a day, while some may be happy with two meals a day. Always take note that snacks should be given in addition to these feedings. Mostly, these are reserved for rewarding and training purposes. Consult your vet about the proper feeding diet for adult and senior Chihuahuas because it can vary depending on your pet's condition or health status.

Tips in Selecting a High-Quality Dog Food Brand

As a pet owner, feeding your pet a high-quality well-balanced food is one of the best things that you can do to keep them healthy. Picking the right food will keep your dog's hair coat sleek and shiny. It will also help strengthen his immune system and it will keep his digestive system in good health.

In order to improve your Chihuahua's diet, start by simply ignoring the labeling claims on commercial pet food.

Look instead for AAFCO certification so that you can be sure it meets the basic requirements for vitamins and trace minerals.

How to Select Dry Pet Foods

The first thing to look in dry pet food is meat. Dogs are carnivores and they thrive on a diet that is based on meat. Dogs do not need a lot of carbohydrates. The reason why grains and carbs are added to pet food is because they are way cheaper than meat, and they hold the kibbled bits together. They didn't add that for the sake of good nutrition for your meat-eating pet.

The quality and source of protein content in the formula are very important for your pet's health. The first thing to look for in a dog's food is the ingredient list like beef, turkey, lamb or chicken. Avoid any formula that makes use of unidentified sources, described non-specifically as meat, animal, or poultry.

How to Feed Your Chihuahua Dogs

Owning a Chihuahua means understanding their feeding requirements. You should be knowledgeable about this because this is very important for their health. At any stage of their lives, they should be given a proper diet to ensure that their body is strong against diseases.

If you are feeding your Chihuahuas in a wrong way, it may result in some health problems. They may suffer from obesity or other diseases like strained ligaments and joints if you feed them too much. Take note that a puppy burns more calories quickly compared to adults. Therefore, it is very vital to understand the food requirement of your Chihuahua depending on his age.

Importance of quality food for your Chihuahuas

Cheap dog foods contain various harmful ingredients which may affect the health of your pet in a negative way. You have to be aware that various harmful by products and fillers are present in different dog foods and these have almost zero nutrition. It is good if you can feed your dog raw food diet. The amount of food given varies on the age, size, metabolism and the level of the activity of your dog.

Recommended daily amount of food to a Chihuahua adult is ¼ to ½ cup of high quality dry food and these are given in two meals.

Below are the recommended servings for puppies, consult your vet if you aren't sure about the proper amount for your Chihuahua:

- ½ cup of food for 1 pound puppy
- 1 cup of food for 3 pounds puppy
- 25 cups of food for 5 pound puppy
- 2 cups of food for 6 pounds puppy

There will be changes to the feeding requirements specifically for pregnant, senior, and inactive Chihuahuas so it is advised that you consult with your vet. Young Chihuahuas burn more calories compared to older breeds because they have high energy levels and require food at regular intervals to aid their growth. A growing Chihuahua should be fed three to four times a day at regular intervals. Again, it is better to consult with your vet because there is no one – size – fits – all diet, feeding amount and frequency will vary.

Toxic Foods to Avoid

There are some foods that you should not feed your Chihuahua under any occasion. The list of foods below should be carefully avoided to keep your dog away from accidents.

- **Alcohol**

  Alcoholic beverages or food products that contain alcohol may cause diarrhea, vomiting, central nervous system depression, decreased coordination, difficulty breathing, abnormal blood acidity, tremors, coma, and even death.

- **Avocado**

  Dogs that might get a chance to eat avocado may cause cardiovascular damage or even death.

- **Chocolate, coffee, and caffeine**

  All of these products contain substances called methylxanthines which can be found in cacao seeds. If these are ingested by dogs, they might experience diarrhea, vomiting, panting, excessive thirst and urination, abnormal heart rhythm, seizures and even death.

- **Citrus**

  This can cause irritation and possibly even central nervous system depression if eaten in significant amounts.

- **Coconut and coconut oil**

  This may not cause serious harm to your pet if ingested in just small amounts. But it may cause stomach upsets, loose stools or diarrhea.

- **Grapes and raisins**

  These fruits can cause kidney failure although it is still not known what substance is present in grapes and raisins. Until more information is known about its toxic substance, it is still best to avoid feeding raisins and grapes to your dogs.

- **Macadamia nuts**

  This can cause weakness, vomiting, depression, tremors and hyperthermia on dogs.

- **Milk and dairy**

  Milk and other dairy products can cause dogs' diarrhea or other digestive problems.

- **Nuts**

  Nuts contain a high amount of oils and fats that can cause vomiting and diarrhea and also pancreatitis in pets.

- **Onions, garlic, chives**

  These herbs and vegetables can cause gastrointestinal irritation that could lead to red blood cell damage.

- **Raw/Undercooked Meat, Eggs, and Bones**

  Raw eggs and meats may contain bacteria like Salmonella and E. coli that can be harmful not only to dogs but also to humans. On the other hand, raw bones can be very dangerous for a domestic pet that might choke on bones.

- **Salt and salty snack foods**

  These can produce excessive thirst and urination, or even sodium ion poisoning for your Chihuahuas which will lead to vomiting, diarrhea, tremors, depression, elevated body temperature, seizures and even death.

- **Xylitol**

  This is used as a sweetener which can cause insulin release in most dogs, which can lead to liver failure.

- **Yeast dough**

  This can cause gas to accumulate in your dog's digestive system that may lead to stomach bloat, and potentially twist that may become a life threatening emergency.

Chapter Six: Maintenance for Chihuahuas

Let's assume that you already have your own Chihuahua dog. The most difficult part of owning one is the responsibility that comes with it. It is necessary to provide them their basic needs and keep them healthy all the time.

In this chapter, you will be informed about how to properly take care of your dog and how to maintain their healthy lifestyle as well as their well-being. If you start it the right way, taking care of these cute creatures will be a breeze!

Tips on How to Dog-Proof Your Home

If you already purchased your Chihuahua, you should keep in mind that you have to provide a safe environment for them. There are steps to be taken to prepare your yard and home for your dog in order to eliminate any dangers. Baby proofing your home is similar to preparing your home for a new puppy. New dogs are impertinent by nature, so they would want to investigate everything even if those things could be dangerous. Therefore, you should make sure that each room of your home is a safe environment for your pet.

Dog proofing bathrooms and kitchens

Bathrooms and kitchens could be dangerous for your pets because of the cleaning supplies, medications, and other chemicals. These are the two basic rooms in your home where dog proofing is imperative. Consider the following to keep your pets safe in the bathrooms and kitchens.

- Make sure to put items like cleaning supplies, laundry soaps and medications on high shelves.
- Keep all the food out of reach from your dogs because it might be dangerous for consumption. Even if the

food does not cause a threat, the packaging could be the problem.

- Always keep trash cans covered so that your dog won't get into the garbage
- Some pets are not only curious but quite clever so consider installing childproof latches on cabinets.
- Avoid your pet from jumping into the dryer before turning it on.
- Block any small spaces such as small spaces behind the washer and dryer or holes in cabinets.
- Always keep the toilet lid down so that your pet can not drink harmful chemicals.

Dog proofing the living room

Not only the kitchen and the bathroom pose most serious threats for pets but also the living room because it contains items that could also be dangerous. In order to make sure that your pets are safe in the living room, you must consider the following:

- Move your plants out of reach from your Chihuahuas and better yet, assure that all plants in your home or yard is safe for your pet and is not poisonous to them.
- Make sure that any heating or air vents have proper covers

- Keep dangling wires from stereos, televisions, lamps and other items out of reach
- Put away from your dogs any breakable items such as knick knacks that your Chihuahua can knock over and break
- Put away any toys or kid games that have small pieces because this can be a choking hazard to your curious but still cute Chihuahua.

Dog proof the bedroom

The bedroom might be safe for your Chihuahuas and not a lot are needed to be done here to dog proof. However, there are still few steps that can be taken to make your bedroom safer for your Chihuahuas:

- Keep any medicine, lotion or cosmetics that are placed on a bedside table, out of reach.
- Make sure that your Chihuahuas cannot get access to any electric wires because they can chew them.
- Keep laundry and shoes out of reach because buttons and strings can pose a choking hazard and potentially even more serious issues if ingested
- Make sure that your Chihuahuas are not staying or sleeping in drawers or closets before shutting them. They are so small you might not notice them, they can die out of suffocation.

Dog proof the garage and backyard

The backyard and the garage can be home to a number of items that are risky for your Chihuahuas just as with the kitchen and bathroom. If you are thinking of leaving your Chihuahuas in the garage and backyard for a few minutes, you must first consider the following:

- Make sure to clean the floor of the garage so that chemicals like antifreeze are nowhere to be found. Your Chihuahua can die if these chemicals are ingested.
- Move all chemicals in the garage to high shelves or in a closet that can't be accessed by your pets.
- Check the fence for any spaces or holes where your Chihuahua might squeeze through and patch them up or consider boarding the spaces.

Habitat Requirements for Chihuahuas

The great thing about Chihuahuas is that they don't take up too much space to roam around with (they can actually fit in a cup!), but aside from space, the main thing your Chihuahua needs in terms of its habitat is lots of love and affection from his human companions and adequate daily exercise. Even though Chihuahuas are sometimes too quite temperamental and a bit witty, it is a very devoted and affectionate breed that bonds closely with family, so you should make an effort to spend some quality time with your Chihuahua each and every day. If you're Chihuahua doesn't get enough attention he may be more likely to develop problem behaviors like chewing or excessive barking and potential aggression as well as separation anxiety – because that is their way for you to notice them!

In addition to playing with your Chihuahua and spending time with him every day, you also need to make sure that his needs for exercise are met. The Chihuahua doesn't require extensive exercises but it is still recommended to take your dog for a walk or run for at least 30 minutes to 1 hour a day plus some active play time. This is very important for your Chihuahua. You should also make sure your Chihuahua gets plenty of mental stimulation from interactive toys and games.

Toys and Accessories for Chihuahuas

Chihuahua supplies will change as each young puppy matures into an adult (but still miniature) dog and also when they become a senior. The products associated with Chihuahua clearly indicate if they're appropriate for their age. When you are already ready to welcome your new pet into your home, make sure you already have their personal supplies stocked to help keep them happy and healthy at every stage of their lives.

With the right nutrients and ingredients, your food supplies can help give your Chihuahuas the building blocks they need to prolong their years of barking and tail wagging. You can also provide your Chihuahua some treats to keep them feeling rewarded, focused and excited to learn new tricks and right manners.

However, if your Chihuahuas aren't pleased by treats, you can give them a collection of dog toys for every preference. In that way, you can have a reward system for your Chihuahua or simply just give them some much needed exercise with their plush dog ball or toys.

In addition to treating and toy fueled playtime, daily walks with your Chihuahuas can provide great bonding moments. When you're out for a walk make sure that your pet's accessories are "Hollywood" quality – because your Chihuahua needs to live up to its reputation! There is a large array of Chihuahua accessories and clothes for every occasion and season to keep them looking comfortably stylish wherever they go.

If your pet is new to walks, there are also specialized dog accessories that are already available to help your pet become trained while on a leash, so you can make sure your young Chihuahua can respect the rules of the road as they explore the world outside of their homes. There are also dog training supplies available in the market to reinforce good behavior like pee pads, clickers, and bark collars.

Additionally, your Chihuahua deserves the best bed or crating dog supplies for their size and sleeping style. Dog crate covers, heated bed products, and blankets can also make for a more comfortable good night's rest.

For your on-the-go needs, there are also dog carriers and car seat accessories available in the market if you want to make trips to the park. Getting the right car accessories for your Chihuahua doesn't just only make you hassle-free during travel, but they will also make it more comfortable and safer too. Also, if your vet prescribes or recommends something for your pup, you must really invest on it like dog products to tackle fleas, ticks, and more.

Tips for Keeping Your Dogs Happy Indoors and Outdoors

Chihuahuas are the total indoor dog that's why they must always be kept inside our homes, in a safely fenced yard, or on-leash. But they are not inside our homes all the time. They can still go for a walk at the dog park provided they have a full supervision. This section will enumerate the tips that will help your dog stay happy whether indoors or outdoors.

Even if they like staying indoors, Chihuahua are also curious as to what's going on outside so why not open the curtains of your homes once in a while or perhaps every day! Most dogs enjoy a nice view, especially when it's sunny outside, the incoming light can improve your dog's mood. Open also the windows so that your Chihuahuas can get some fresh air. Just make sure to do this only if you are at home and there's someone looking after your Chihuahua. Puzzle games are also great for a dog while they are indoors. It can be a nice pass time and can stimulate your dog's brain especially if you are not always there to play with them.

You can also try buying a treadmill for your Chihuahuas. It can be a great way to keep your dog in good shape when you have no time to exercise them. Your dog then can definitely exercise at home where it's convenient if ever you got sick or if the weather is bad. Having a bond with your dog indoors is the best thing to do when you can't go outside for a walk. Make sure to always make time for your Chihuahuas. You may snuggle on the couch, make a brushing session, or even a massage will definitely keep them happy.

You can also practice training your dog when you are inside your homes. Although it may seem boring, your Chihuahua might enjoy this because it gives them a job and they are getting to work with you. Taking even just a small amount of time to practice tricks, obedience, etc. will keep your dog's mind sharp and will eliminate boredom.

As mentioned earlier, Chihuahua dogs are intended indoors so it is not really recommended that he should be treated as an outdoor dog, even though he can moderately tolerate the hot and cold weather. It's better off leaving him inside your home with your family.

You can let your pet go outdoors like in the yard when he is already a bit older or well – trained inside. However, make sure that there are no other dogs that can get in and this includes other dogs you own (unless they are properly introduced).

If you want to let them hang outside, your yard should be clean and the ground should be treated for weeds and fleas. When your Chihuahua reached around eight weeks old, you can take them outside as long as you supervise them at all times.

You must avoid taking your Chihuahuas out in public areas until his puppy shots are already completed. This includes walking along the footpath, being out in your front yard, at the shops, in parks, in yards belonging to neighbours and so on. Your dog must be 12 - 16 weeks old before he can be safely taken outdoors, be sure to put him on a leash.

It's very unhealthy to keep your dog indoors at all times. Your home won't have sufficient space for him to roam around unless you have a spacious mansion. It is necessary to give your Chihuahuas a significant amount of sunshine each day for Vitamin D. Besides, getting enough exercise for your Chihuahua is very essential. You have to plan your walks the same time each day so that he has something to look forward to. Exercises are important because it helps him get off diseases and he could be able to smell, hear and see new things. This can make his heart healthy and balances out his muscle tone. The most important thing at the end of the day is that you get to bond with your pet.

Chapter Seven: Showing Your Chihuahuas

    The Chihuahua is a wonderful dog to keep as a pet but this breed has the potential to be so much more than that. These dogs are very intelligent, active, trainable and super competitive compare to other miniature dog breeds which makes them a great choice as a show dog. In order to show your Chihuahua, however, you have to make sure that he meets the requirements for the breed standard and you need to learn the basics about showing dogs. In this chapter you will receive information about the breed standard for Chihuahua breeds and you will find general information about preparing your dog for show.

Chihuahua Breed Standard

The Chihuahua is an alert, clever and enthusiastic breed that is accepted and recognized by the American Kennel Club (AKC). This section will give you the breed standard and general guidelines on how to present your dog.

Official Chihuahua Standard

General Appearance: the body must be compact; must be graceful, active and alert, swift – moving and should have terrier – like temperament and saucy impression.

Height: 15 – 23 cm (5 – 9 inches) tall

Temperament: should project confidence, self – reliance, grace yet alert, and self - importance

Head: The skull should be shaped like an "apple dome," with or without molera.

Eyes: must be round but not protruding; must be balanced on both sides and set well – apart; must have light eyes in blond or white – colored Chihuahuas. If your dog has blue eyes or has a different color in the iris of its two eyes or there are two different colors in one iris, it will be considered a major fault.

Ears: It must be erect, large and held more upright when alert but must be flaring at a 45 degree angle when in repose; must be well – defined; when it is viewed in profile, the ears form a near 90 degree angle where muzzle joins skull.

Muzzle: Must be moderately short and slightly pointed; cheeks and jaws should be lean

Nose: Must be self – colored in blond or black Chihuahuas; in moles, blues and chocolates – they should also be self – colored. Pink – noses are permissible in blond types. It is disqualified if your dog's ears are cropped or broken down.

Bite: Must be level or scissors; it is permissible if your dog is missing a tooth or two.

Neck: must be slightly arched and sloping into lean shoulders

Topline: should be leveled

Body Structure: the ribs should be well – sprung and rounded (should not be "barrel – shaped")

Tail: must be moderately long; should be carried sickle either up or out or in a loop over the back with the tip touching its back. It will be disqualified, if your dog has a docked tail, bobtail or it's tucked between the legs.

Forequarters: the shoulders must be lean, and it must slope into a broadening support above straight forelegs that will give free movement at the elbows. Shoulders should be well – up giving balance that slopes into a level back, giving it a well – develop chest and strong forequarters. The feet in front should be small and dainty with toes being well split up but not spread; the pads must be cushioned the pasterns must be strong; the dewclaws could be removed.

Hindquarters: must be muscular with hock well apart (neither in nor out). It should be firm and sturdy. It should be equal to that of forequarters, same with the feet; the dewclaws could be removed.

Coat Quality: For Smooth or Short – Coated Chihuahuas it must be soft, close and glossy; the coat should be well – place over the body with ruff on the neck being preferred as well as more scanty on its head and ears. The hair on its tail should be furry. For Long – Coated Chihuahuas, the coat should also be soft, either flat or a bit wavy, with undercoat preferred. The hairs in the ears should be fringed, while the hairs in its tail should be full and long. Must have a feathering hair on its feet and legs; pants on its hind legs and preferably a large ruff on its neck. It will be disqualified, if the coat is too thin (almost resembling bareness).

Coat Colors: Must be solid, marked or splashed

Gait: should have a swift movement, must be firm and sturdy. From the rear, the hocks must be parallel to each other; the foot fall of the rear legs follows behind the forelegs. The topline must be firm and backline level as your Chihuahua moves.

Disqualifications: A Chihuahua that weighs more than 6 pounds; a dog with broken down or cropped ears; docked tail or bobtail; a too thin coat for long – coated Chihuahuas

Tips on Preparing Your Chihuahua for Show

Once you've determined that your Chihuahua achieved all the requirements of the breed standard, and then you can think about entering him in a dog show. Dog shows occur all year-round in many different locations so check the AKC or Kennel Club website for shows in your area. Remember, the rules for each show will be different so make sure to do your research so that you and your Chihuahua are properly prepared for the show.

Here are some things you need to keep in mind while prepping your dog for show:

- Make sure that your Chihuahua has been housetrained completely before registering him for a show.

- Ensure that your dog is properly socialized to be in an environment with many other dogs and people.

- Make sure that your Chihuahua has had at least basic obedience training. He needs to respond to your commands and follow your lead in the show ring.

- Research the requirements for the individual show and make sure your pet meets them before you register.

- Take your dog to the vet to ensure that he is healthy enough for show and that he is caught up on his vaccinations; the bordatella vaccine is especially important since he'll be around a lot of other dogs.

- Pack a bag of supplies for things that you and your dog are likely to need at the show.

- Have your Chihuahua groomed on or before the week of the show and take steps to make sure his coat stays in good condition.

Quick Checklist

Here are some things that may come in handy before, during and after the show:

- Registration information
- Dog crate or exercise pen
- Grooming table and grooming supplies
- Food and treats
- Food and water bowls
- Trash bags
- Medication (if needed)
- Change of clothes
- Food/water for self
- Paper towels or rags
- Toys for the dog

Chapter Eight: Breeding Your Chihuahuas

Do want to bred and raise Chihuahuas on your own? Well, this chapter for you! However, you have to consider questions such as; do you have the financial capacity to support lots of puppies? This is because breeding involves many vet bills, food supplies, and other dog needs. The next major question is do you have time to take care of these newborns? Newborn puppies may require 'round the clock supervision and maintenance as they grow. Read on if you really want to become a breeder, but do take note that there are a lot of things that you should know. This chapter will give you an idea on how to breed Chihuahuas.

Basic Dog Breeding Information

The first rule that to you have to understand and follow is that breeding is best left to professional breeders. But of course, it is also essential that you know the basics of breeding a dog. A lot of things are involved, and it is important that you know your responsibilities and all the things that you need to observe to ensure that the breeding will produce healthy Chihuahua puppies.

There is somewhat a high level of loss in puppies. This is caused by different kinds of reasons, and can also happen in any breed not only on Chihuahua, but this happens more often in toy breeds. Anyone who is breeding must understand and accept that puppies may die inexplicably at times. It is heartbreaking and tragic of course.

Mating

When a female dog or what they termed it as the 'bitch' is in heat, there are a few signs that can point towards her beginning this process. These are:

- Being nervous
- Easily spooked
- Easily distracted
- Urinating more than usual

Her personality may also alter due to the abrupt change in her hormones. Male dogs in general are ready to breed from the age of 18 months to 4/5 years old. An interesting fact about male dogs is that when they hit the age around 10 years old, the semen they produce will not be capable of impregnating a female.

Ovulation Timing

A lot of breeders today use lab tests to measure Progesterone, vaginal cytology, and luteinizing hormone to determine when ovulation occurs. Breeders know that the cycle is usually 21 days despite what some male dogs think. What may be normal for one dog may differ from another. Some bitches' cycle on schedule, while others mate and ovulate from 12-21 days. Some have 'clear heats,' false or flaky seasons, or even false pregnancies. Here are the average estrus changes an owner may expect in normal heat cycles.

- **Day 1:** Attention to rear and licking. Discharge is bright or dark red color, swelling of the vulva. You can start counting heat cycle from when the blood hits the ground.

- **Day 2 – 7:** Bright red discharge with swelling increases

- **Day 8 – 10:** The color begins to lighten and turn into pinkish. Swelling is at peak and the vulva has a spongy feel and look.

- **Day 9 – 14:** The color changes from light pink to clear or straw colored. The swelling is down and the vulva may appear hard or dry on edges.

- **Day 14 – 21:** Color clears, discharge and swelling is almost gone and bitch may already act receptive, but is still snappy. You can count 58 - 62 days for puppies! But there also exceptions to the rule. Some bitched may mate and conceive as late as 22 days.

Tips for Breeding Your Chihuahuas

Now that you know the basics about breeding dogs you can learn the specifics about Chihuahuas. The Chihuahuas has a gestation period lasting about 58 - 68 days (or about 9 to 10 weeks). The gestation period is the period of time following conception during which the puppies develop in the mother's uterus. The average litter size for the Chihuahua breed is between 1 to 3 puppies, some Chihuahuas can reach a maximum of 7 – 10 newborns. Keep in mind that new mothers will often have smaller litters –

the next few litters will generally be larger before the litter size starts to taper off again.

To increase your chances of a successful breeding, you need to keep track of your Chihuahua's estrus cycle. Once your female reaches the point of ovulation, you can introduce her to the male dog and let nature take its course. Breeding behavior varies slightly from one breed to another, but you can expect the male dog to mount the female from behind (as long as she is receptive). If the breeding is successful, conception will occur and the gestation period will begin.

While the puppies are developing inside your female Chihuahua's uterus, you need to take special care to make sure the female is properly nourished. You do not need to make changes to your dog's diet until the fourth or fifth week of pregnancy. At that point you should slightly increase her daily rations in an amount proportionate to her weight gain. It is generally best to offer your dog free feeding because she will know how much she needs to eat. Make sure your dog's diet is high in protein as well as calories and fat to support the development of her puppies – calcium is also very important.

Labor Process of Chihuahuas

By the eighth week of pregnancy you should start preparing yourself and your dog for the whelping. This is the time when you should set up a whelping box where your female dog can comfortably give birth to her puppies. Place the box in a quiet, dim area and line it with newspapers and old towels for comfort. The closer it gets to the whelping, the more time your dog will spend in the whelping box, preparing it for her litter.

During the last week of your Chihuahua's pregnancy you should start taking her internal temperature at least once per day – this is the greatest indicator of impending labor. The normal body temperature for a dog is about 100°F to 102°F (37.7°C to 38.8°C). When your dog's body temperature drops, you can expect contractions to begin within 24 hours or so. Prior to labor, your dog's body temperature may drop as low as 98°F (36.6°C) – if it gets any lower, contact your veterinarian.

Once your Chihuahua starts going into labor, you can expect her to show some obvious signs of discomfort. Your dog might start pacing restlessly, panting, and switching positions. The early stages of labor can often last for several hours and contractions may occur as often as 10 minutes apart. If your pet has contractions for more than 2 hours without any of the puppies being born, contact your veterinarian immediately. Once your dog starts giving birth, the puppies will arrive about every thirty minutes following ten to thirty minutes of straining.

After each puppy is born, the Chihuahua will lick the puppy clean; it may even eat the umbilical cord because it is animal instinct. This also helps to stimulate the puppy to start breathing on his own. Once all of the puppies have been born, the mother will expel the rest of the placenta (the afterbirth) and then let the puppies start nursing. It is essential that the puppies begin nursing within one hour of being born because this is when they will receive the colostrum from the mother. Colostrum is the first milk produced and it contains a variety of nutrients as well as antibodies to protect the pups until their own immune systems have time to develop. In addition to making sure that the puppies are feeding, you should also make sure that the mother eats soon after whelping.

Chihuahua puppies are very small in size since it is a toy breed. As the puppies grow, they will start to become increasingly active and the will grow very quickly as long as they are properly fed by the mother (and by you). The Chihuahua puppies' ears are dropped when they were young, once they reach maturity their ears will naturally be erect.

At six weeks of age is the time you should begin weaning the puppies by offering them small amounts of puppy food soaked in water or broth. The puppies might sample small bits of solid food even while they are still nursing and the mother will general wean the puppies by the eight week, with or without your help. If you plan to sell the puppies, be sure not to send them home unless they are fully weaned at least 8 weeks old. You should also take steps to start socializing the puppies from an early age to make sure they turn into well - adjusted adults.

Chapter Nine: Keeping Your Dog Healthy

As mentioned earlier, Chihuahuas are healthy in general but they are still pre – dispose to certain illnesses and conditions. You as the owner should be aware of the potential threats and diseases that could harm the wellness of your Chihuahuas. Just like human beings, you need to have knowledge on these diseases so that you can prevent it from happening in the first place. In this section, you will find tons of tips on how to maintain your dog happy and healthy. Information about common health problems is also addressed in this section.

Common Health Problems

In this section, you will learn about the diseases that may affect and threaten your Chihuahua's wellness. Learning these diseases as well as its remedies is vital for you and your dog so that you could prevent it from happening or even help with its treatment in case they caught one. You will also learn some guidelines on how these diseases can be prevented and treated as well as its signs and symptoms.

The following are the most common health problems of the Chihuahua breed:

- Hydrocephalus
- Hypoglycemia
- Patellar Luxation
- Tracheal Collapse
- Obesity
- Heart Conditions
- Hip Dysplasia
- Cataracts

Hydrocephalus

Chihuahuas are born with a soft spot on their heads called Molera. If your dog has an enlarge molera, he or she may be suffering from hydrocephalus. This condition occurs when fluids around the brain builds up, which could result in fatality.

The common symptoms you need to watch out for are the following:

- swollen head

- listlessness

- lethargy

- grogginess

- poor coordination

- seizures

This condition usually affects Chihuahuas 9 months old and below, some dogs may not show symptoms until it's too late. However, there are also some Chihuahuas who survive well into their adulthood despite suffering from a mild case of hydrocephalus.

Hypoglycemia

This health issue is occurs when there is a sudden drop in blood sugar levels. This can be very dangerous and sometimes can be fatal. This commonly happens to puppies under the age of 3 months old.

The blood sugar insufficiency can lead to major conditions such as insulinoma, Insulin overdose and Addison's disease.

Here are the symptoms you need to look out for in case your Chihuahua is suffering from Hypoglycemia:

- Muscle incoordination
- Confusion and disorientation
- Seizures
- Nervousness
- Lethargy and weakness
- Restlessness and agitation
- Trembling

Collapsed Trachea

This is also common to Chihuahua dogs. Some of this may be because of genetics, but this can be prevented in most cases. The trachea or the windpipe is supported by rings that are made up of cartilage. This cartilage is prone to injury with toy breeds. With regards to trauma related collapsed trachea, it is often due to the use of a collar instead of harness. You can use a supplement with glucosamine for your Chihuahua to keep its joints moist, smooth and healthy.

Patellar Luxation in Dogs

Patellar luxation is another common disease in toy and miniature dog breeds. This occurs when the dog's kneecap (patella) is dislocated from its normal anatomic position in the groove of the thigh bone (femur). Female dogs are usually the ones affected by these disease more than male dogs.

When the kneecap is dislocated from the groove of the thigh bone, it can only be returned to its normal position once the quadriceps muscles in the hind legs of the animal relax and lengthen. It is for this reason that most dogs with the condition will hold up their hind legs for a few minutes.

The main cause of patellar luxation or a dislocated kneecap is genetic malformation or trauma. This condition can normally be seen approximately four months after birth. Usually, a dog with a dislocated kneecap will exhibit prolonged abnormal hind limb movement, occasional skipping or hind limb lameness, and sudden lameness. The specific symptoms of a dislocated kneecap will depend on the severity and persistence of the condition, as well as the amount of degenerative arthritis that is involved.

Veterinarians will usually suggest performing Craniocaudal (top view) and Mediolateral (side view) X-rays for the stifle joint, hip, and hock as well as skyline X-rays for the thigh bone. Your vet will also likely perform an examination by touch to feel for kneecap freedom.The Craniocaudal and Mediolateral tests will detect the bending and twisting of the thigh bone and larger bone of the lower leg while Skyline X-rays may reveal a shallow, flattened, or curved groove of the thigh bone.

Aside from X-rays, a fluid sample may also be taken from the joint and an analysis of the lubricating fluid in the joint may show a small increase in mononuclear cells.

Obesity

Obesity is also very common among toy breeds, and sometimes the main cause is you! Owners enjoy feeding these adorable dogs but most of the time; it results to you over – feeding them. Obesity shortens their life expectancy and it could also lead them vulnerable to other diseases such as diabetes. The only way to prevent this is to make sure that you feed your pet the right amount and also encourage them to exercise every day.

Hip Dysplasia

Hip dysplasia is a very common musculoskeletal problem among miniature dogs. In a normal hip, the part of the thigh bone sits snugly within the groove of the hip joint and it rotates freely within the grove as the dog moves. Hip dysplasia occurs when the femoral head becomes separated from the hip joint – this is called subluxation. This could occur as a result of abnormal joint structure or laxity in the muscles and ligaments supporting the joint. This condition can present in pups as young as 5 months of age or in older dogs.

Cataracts

Canine cataracts are the most common problems affecting the dog's eye. Toy dogs, like the Chihuahuas are also prone to this sickness. This health issue can appear at any age from when the Chihuahua is born up until he becomes older.

Recommended Vaccinations for Chihuahuas

All dogs, including Chihuahua need shots or vaccinations to help prevent diseases and make their body's immune system stronger. Your vet will be making a recommendation, but normally, your Chihuahua will get these general vaccines similar to other dog breed.

Puppy shots

Never neglect to get your Chihuahua a shot even if it seems that he is too small to have one because this is vital to their health. Chihuahua puppies first get their shots as soon as they leave their moms. If you get your dog from a breeder at eight to nine weeks old, it is assumed that he already got a shot – even six –week- old puppies can be given a vaccination.

When puppies get boosters, they get a natural immunity from their moms but it interferes with the shots that you gave to them. The best thing to do is give your Chihuahua puppy a series of shots to make sure he's covered when he needs it. Chihuahua should be getting boosters every two to four weeks until he's 16 weeks old. As soon as he is finished with puppy shots, give your Chihuahua a booster shots once every three years but if your vet recommends annual boosters, follow it and go with that schedule.

Below table summarizes the different vaccinations that can be given to your Chihuahua. You can review it so you have an idea what shots to give to your dogs. In this section you will learn the vaccination schedule that your puppy or dog may need, but be sure to consult the veterinarian for further instructions.

Vaccination Schedule for Dogs			
Vaccine	**Doses**	**Age**	**Booster**
Rabies	1	12 weeks	annual
Distemper	3	6-16 weeks	3 years
Parvovirus	3	6-16 weeks	3 years
Adenovirus	3	6-16 weeks	3 years
Parainfluenza	3	6 weeks, 12-14 weeks	3 years
Bordatella	1	6 weeks	annual
Lyme Disease	2	9, 13-14 weeks	annual
Leptospirosis	2	12 and 16 weeks	annual
Canine Influenza	2	6-8, 8-12 weeks	annual

Signs of Possible Illnesses

- **Sneezing** - does your dog have nose discharge?
- **Dehydration** -does your dog drink less than the usual? It may be a sign that there is something wrong with your dog
- **Obesity** -is your dog showing signs of obesity? It may be prone to a heart disease, or diabetes. Monitor your dog's weight before it's too late.
- **Elimination** -does your dog regularly urinate and defecate? Always check its litter to make sure that its stool and urine is normal. Contact the vet immediately if there are any signs of bleed and diarrhea.
- **Vomiting** - does your dog vomits and is it showing signs of appetite loss?
- **Coat** -does its coat and skin still feel soft, firm and rejuvenated? If your dog is sick sometimes, it appears physically on its body.
- **Paws/Limbs** -does your dog have trouble walking or is it only dragging its legs? It could be a sign of paralysis.
- **Eyes** - are there any discharge in the eyes?
- **Overall Physique** - does your dog stays active or are there any signs of weakness and deterioration?

Emergency Guide

Accidents do happen and we cannot avoid them. When there are medical emergencies that befall our dogs, owners may find it difficult to make rational decisions, especially when it occurs in the middle of the night. That is why it is very important that we know what to do and should have an emergency plan in place – before we need it.

Signs Your Pet May Need Emergency Care

There are a lot of reasons when your dog needs an emergency care like a severe trauma – caused by accident or fall – choking, insect sting, heatstroke, household poisoning or other life – threatening circumstances. Below are some signs that emergency care is necessary.

- Pale gums
- Rapid breathing
- Weak or rapid pulse
- Change in body temperature
- Difficulty standing
- Apparent paralysis

- Loss of consciousness

- Seizures

- Excessive bleeding

What to do

Dogs that are severely injured may be aggressive toward their owners, so it is very important to first protect yourself from injury.

Approach your dog calmly and slowly, kneel down and say his name. If the dog is aggressive, call for immediate help. If he is passive, fashion a makeshift stretcher and gently carry him onto it. Be sure to support his neck and back in case he is suffering any spinal injuries.

First Aid Treatments

A lot of medical emergencies require immediate veterinary care, but first aid methods may help in stabilizing your pet for transportation.

- If the dog is suffering from bleeding because of trauma, try to elevate and apply pressure to the wound
- If your pet is choking, place your fingers inside his mouth and see if you can remove the blockage

- If you cannot remove the foreign object, perform a modified Heimlich maneuver by giving a sharp rap to his chest which will dislodge the object.

Performing CPR on your Pet

CPR may be important if your pet remains unconscious after you have removed the object that chokes him. Check first to see if he is still breathing. If not, place him on his side and perform an artificial respiration by extending his neck and head, holding his jaws closed and by blowing into his nostrils once every 3 seconds. Be sure that no air escapes between your mouth and the nose of your pet. If you really cannot hear a heartbeat, incorporate a cardiac massage, while having artificial respiration – three quick, firm chest compression for every respiration until your dog can breath normally already.

Pet Poisoning

If you think your Chihuahua has ingested a toxic food or substance, call your vet immediately or the ASPCA Animal Poison Control Center's 24-hour hotline at (888) 426 – 4435. They will make a recommendation, and will consider the age and health of your dog and what and how he ate. It may include inducing vomiting based on their assessment.

Chapter Ten: Chihuahua Care Sheet

Yay! You have made it this far! Now, you have all the information that you need in becoming a well-informed dog owner. All the information that you have read will help you in being the best owner that you can be for your new pet. I'm sure you are excited for the next chapter of your life with your superbly cute Chihuahua after reading this book. You are now well on your way in becoming an official pet owner!

This chapter contains a summary of everything that you have read and learned from this book. The sassy Chihuahuas are waiting for you!

Chihuahua Information Sheet

Pedigree: Toy Breed

Breed Size: Small

Height: 15 – 23 cm (5 – 9 inches) tall

Weight: weighs 1.5 – 3 kg (3 – 6 pounds)

Types: Smooth-Coat Chihuahua; Long-Coat Chihuahua; Apple Head Chihuahua; Deer Head Chihuahua; Teacup Chihuahua; Fawn Chihuahua

Coat Texture: may be smooth and silky

Color: Tan, Red, Black, White or Splashed

Eyes: bulging eyes that is dark and expressive

Ears: erect ears when matured or full grown; drop ears when younger

Tail: erect and curled up; about 3 - 5 inches in length

Temperament: can be easily trained, intelligent, tenacious, active, loyal, sweet

Strangers: sociable when trained well, but are not that welcoming.

Other Dogs: proper socialization is needed. They could have barking tendencies and also tend to always throw themselves at larger dogs

Other Pets: generally not good with other pets

Training: Highly trainable

Exercise Needs: requires minimum exercise and play time with the use of lively activities; about 30 minutes to about an hour a day

Health Conditions: generally healthy but may be prone to certain health conditions such as Hydrocephalus, Hypoglycemia, Patellar Luxation, Tracheal Collapse, Obesity, Hip Dysplasia and Cataracts

Lifespan: average 12 - 18 years or more

Chihuahua's Habitat Requirements

Recommended Accessories: dog bed, food/water dishes, toys, collar, leash, harness, grooming supplies

Collar and Harness: size by weight

Grooming: low maintenance

Energy Level: very high energy level

Exercise Requirements: 30 minutes to 1 hour a day of training, walking and playing

Food/Water: uses stainless steel or ceramic bowls, clean daily

Toys: start with an assortment to check which the dog likes

Chihuahua's Nutritional Needs

Nutritional Needs: water, protein, carbohydrate, fats, vitamins, minerals

Important Ingredients: fresh animal protein (chicken, beef, lamb, turkey, eggs), digestible carbohydrates (rice, oats, barley), animal fats

Types of Food: Wet, Soft and Moist or Dry Food

Amount or Frequency: varies depending on age, size and weight (refer to Chapter 5)

Important Minerals: calcium, phosphorus, potassium, magnesium, iron, copper and manganese

Important Vitamins: Vitamin A, Vitamin A, Vitamin B-12, Vitamin D, Vitamin C

Look For: AAFCO statement of nutritional adequacy; protein at top of ingredients list; no artificial flavors, dyes, preservatives

Breeding Information

Age of First Heat: 6 months old, sometimes earlier or later by a few months

Heat (Estrus) Cycle: 14 to 21 days

Gestation Period: 59 to 63 days

Pregnancy Detection: possible after 21 days, best to wait 28-30 days before exam

Puppies: born with eyes and ears closed; eyes open at 3 weeks, teeth develop at 10 weeks

Litter Size: average of 1 - 3 puppies

Weaning: supplement with controlled portions of moistened puppy food at around 4 weeks, or when the mother starts losing interest in feeding the puppies. Fully weaned at 7 - 8 weeks

Socialization: start as early as possible to prevent puppies from being nervous as an adult, preferably before 14-16 weeks of age

Index

A

B

C

D

I

K

L

M

Photo Credits

References

"6 Different Types of Chihuahua Dog Breeds" Teacup Dog Daily
<https://www.teacupdogdaily.com/types-chihuahua-list/>

"Chihuahua" Dogtime.com
<http://dogtime.com/dog-breeds/chihuahua#/slide/1>

"Chihuahua" Vetstreet.com
<http://www.vetstreet.com/dogs/chihuahua>

"Chihuahua" Pethealth101.com

<http://www.pethealth101.com/breeds/chihuahua.shtml>

"Chihuahua (dog)" Wikipedia.org
<https://en.wikipedia.org/wiki/Chihuahua_(dog)>

"Chihuahua Dog Breed" Petmd.com

<http://www.petmd.com/dog/breeds/c_dg_chihuahua>

"Chihuahua: Graceful, Charming, Sassy" AKC.org
<http://www.akc.org/dog-breeds/chihuahua/>

"Chihuahua Health" Totally Chihuahuas
<http://www.totallychihuahuas.com/health-nutrition/chihuahua-health>
"Chihuahua Health Problems" Natural – dog – health – remedies.com

http://www.natural-dog-health-remedies.com/chihuahua-health-problems.html

"Chihuahua History" Totally Chihuahuas
<http://www.totallychihuahuas.com/history-of-chihuahua>

"Chihuahua Official Breed Standard" AKC.org
<http://images.akc.org/pdf/breeds/standards/Chihuahua.pdf
?_ga=2.13042871.144477315.1494514402-
186202706.1485301797>

"Chihuahua Temperament: What's Good About 'Em, What's
Bad About 'Em" YourPureBredPuppy.com
<http://www.yourpurebredpuppy.com/reviews/chihuahuas.
html>

"Crate Training" American Dog Trainers Network

<http://inch.com/~dogs/cratetraining.html>

"Dog Behavior Training – Proven Techniques to Help Solve
Problem Behaviors" Dog Training Central

<http://www.dog-obedience-training-review.com/dog-
behavior-training.html>

"Dog Nutrition Tips" ASPCA

<http://www.aspca.org/pet-care/dog-care/dog-nutrition-
tips>

"Estrus Cycle in Dogs" VCA

<http://www.vcahospitals.com/main/pet-health-
information/article/animal-health/estrus-cycles-in-
dogs/5778>

"Feeding Dogs: Guide to the Small Dog Diet"

Small Dog Place

<http://www.smalldogplace.com/feeding-dogs.html>

"Getting Started Showing Your Dog" AKC

<http://www.akc.org/events/conformation-dog-
    shows/getting-started-showing/>

"Health Issues and Problems in the Chihuahua Dog Breed"
FamousChihuahua.com

<http://www.famouschihuahua.com/chihuahua-health-
problems/>

"Housebreaking (Potty Training) for Puppies and Adult
 Dogs" Michele Welton
    <http://www.yourpurebredpuppy.com/training/articles/do
    g-housebreaking.html>

 "How to Break 7 Common Bad Dog Habits"

Shayna Meliker, VetStreet

<http://www.vetstreet.com/our-pet-experts/how-to-break-7-
    common-bad-dog-habits>

"How to Choose a Good Puppy (Picking the Best Puppy in a
Litter)" Michele Welton
<http://www.yourpurebredpuppy.com/buying/articles/how-
to-choose-a-puppy.html>

"How to Choose an Experienced Dog Breeder" PetMD

<http://www.petmd.com/dog/care/evr_dg_breeders>

"How to Choose High-Quality Dog Food" Alphadog

<https://alphadogfood.com/choose-high-quality-dog-food>

"How to Find a Responsible Dog Breeder" The Humane
Society of the United States

<http://www.humanesociety.org/issues/puppy_mills/tips/fin
ding_responsible_dog_breeder.html?referrer=https://www.g
oogle.com/>

"Knee Problems in Your Dog: Patellar Luxation – Luxating
Kneecaps" 2ndchance.info./Ronald Hines
<http://www.2ndchance.info/patella.htm>

"Legg-Calve-Perthes disease" UPEI

<http://discoveryspace.upei.ca/cidd/disorder/legg-calvé-
    perthes-disease>

"Legg-Calve-Perthes Disease in Dogs" PetMD

<http://www.petmd.com/dog/conditions/musculoskeletal/c_
    dg_legg_calve_perthes_disease>

"Luxating Patella" Race Foster, DVM.
<http://www.peteducation.com/article.cfm?c=2+2084&aid=45
7>

"New to Dog Showing?" The Kennel Club

<http://www.thekennelclub.org.uk/activities/dog-showing/new-to-dog-showing/>

"Owning a Dog Cost" Costhelper

<http://pets.costhelper.com/owning-dog.html>

"People Foods to Avoid Feeding Your Pets" ASPCA

<http://www.aspca.org/pet-care/animal-poison-control/people-foods-avoid-feeding-your-pets>

"Preparing for a dog show" Your Dog
<http://www.yourdog.co.uk/Dog-Activities/preparing-for-a-dog-show.html>

"Puppy proofing basics" Wendy Wilson
<https://www.cesarsway.com/dog-care/puppies/puppy-proofing-basics>

"Responsible Breeding" AKC

<http://www.akc.org/dog-breeders/responsible-breeding/>

"Routine Vaccinations for Puppies and Dogs" WebMD

<http://pets.webmd.com/dogs/guide/routine-vaccinations-puppies-dogs>

"Sleeping Arrangement for New Puppy" BFF Dog Training LLC

<http://www.bfftraining.com/available-puppies/puppy-
    behavior-problems/sleeping-arrangement-for-new-
    puppy/>

"Socializing Your Puppy or Adult Dog to Get Along With the World" Michele Welton
<http://www.yourpurebredpuppy.com/training/articles/dog-
socializing.html>

"Ten Tips for Showing Your Dog" Kelly Roper
<http://dogs.lovetoknow.com/dog-information/ten-tips-
showing-your-dog>

"Thinking of Buying a Puppy? Find a Responsible Breeder." AKC

<http://www.akc.org/press-center/facts-stats/responsible-
    breeders/>

"Tips for Choosing a Healthy Puppy" Susan Koranki
<http://www.fidosavvy.com/choosing-a-healthy-
puppy.html>

"Vaccinations for Your Pet" ASPCA

<http://www.aspca.org/pet-care/general-pet-
    care/vaccinations-your-pet>

"Vaccination Schedule for Dogs and Puppies" PetEducation
<http://www.peteducation.com/article.cfm?c=2+2115&aid=95
0>

"Vaccinating Your Pet" RSPCA
<https://www.rspca.org.uk/adviceandwelfare/pets/general/v
accinating>

"Weaning Puppies" Race Foster, DVM.
<http://www.peteducation.com/article.cfm?c=2+1651&aid=88
7>

"Weaning Puppies from their Mother" PetMD
<http://www.petmd.com/dog/puppycenter/nutrition/evr_dg
_weaning_puppies_from_their_mother#>

"Weaning Puppies: What to Do" WebMD
<http://pets.webmd.com/dogs/weaning-puppies-what-do>

"Where Should My Puppy Sleep?" Katarina
<http://doglifetraining.com/2012/08/where-should-my-
puppy-sleep/

Feeding Baby
Cynthia Cherry
978-1941070000

Axolotl
Lolly Brown
978-0989658430

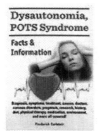

Dysautonomia, POTS
Syndrome
Frederick Earlstein
978-0989658485

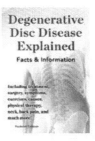

Degenerative Disc
Disease Explained
Frederick Earlstein
978-0989658485

Sinusitis, Hay Fever,
Allergic Rhinitis Explained
Frederick Earlstein
978-1941070024

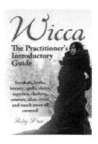

Wicca
Riley Star
978-1941070130

Zombie Apocalypse
Rex Cutty
978-1941070154

Capybara
Lolly Brown
978-1941070062

Eels As Pets
Lolly Brown
978-1941070167

Scabies and Lice Explained
Frederick Earlstein
978-1941070017

Saltwater Fish As Pets
Lolly Brown
978-0989658461

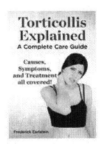

Torticollis Explained
Frederick Earlstein
978-1941070055

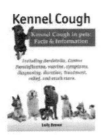

Kennel Cough
Lolly Brown
978-0989658409

Physiotherapist, Physical
Therapist
Christopher Wright
978-0989658492

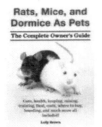

Rats, Mice, and Dormice
As Pets
Lolly Brown
978-1941070079

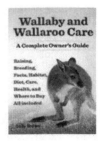

Wallaby and Wallaroo Care
Lolly Brown
978-1941070031

Bodybuilding Supplements
Explained
Jon Shelton
978-1941070239

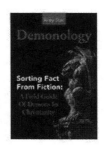

Demonology
Riley Star
978-19401070314

Pigeon Racing
Lolly Brown
978-1941070307

Dwarf Hamster
Lolly Brown
978-1941070390

Cryptozoology
Rex Cutty
978-1941070406

Eye Strain
Frederick Earlstein
978-1941070369

Inez The Miniature Elephant
Asher Ray
978-1941070353

Vampire Apocalypse
Rex Cutty
978-1941070321

Made in the USA
Las Vegas, NV
18 December 2020

14052660R00081